# GOOD SPORTSMANSHIP

by Janet Riehecky
illustrated by Christina Rigo

THE CHILD'S WORLD

Mankato, MN 56001

The sneer is gone from Casey's lip;
   his teeth are clenched in hate;
He pounds with cruel violence
   his bat upon the plate.
And now the pitcher holds the ball,
   and now he lets it go,
And now the air is shattered
   by the force of Casey's blow.

Oh! somewhere in this favored land
   the sun is shining bright;
The band is playing somewhere,
   and somewhere hearts are light.
And somewhere men are laughing,
   and somewhere children shout;
But there is no joy in Mudville—
   mighty Casey has Struck Out.

*—from "Casey at the Bat"*
*by Ernest Lawrence Thayer*

*Verses from "Casey at the Bat"*
*Reprinted with permission of The San Francisco Examiner.*
  *©1989 The San Francisco Examiner.*

**Library of Congress Cataloging in Publication Data**

Riehecky, Janet, 1953-
  Good sportsmanship / by Janet Riehecky ; illustrated by Christina
Rigo.
     p. cm. — (Values to live by)
  Summary: Defines good sportsmanship by presenting situations in
which it is important to be a good sport.
  ISBN 0-89565-563-2
  1. Sportsmanship—Juvenile literature.  [1. Sportsmanship.
2. Conduct of life.]  I. Rigo, Christina Ljungren, ill.  II. Title.
III. Series.
GV706.3.R54   1990
175—dc20                       89-29663
                                     CIP
                                     AC

What is good sportsmanship? Good
sportsmanship is <u>keeping your temper</u>
if you strike out.

When you let the littlest kid on the block have a chance to pitch, that's good sportsmanship.

So is not getting angry with him when
he gives up a home run.

Good sportsmanship is giving your
friend a second chance . . .

and not making fun of her if she
misses again.

If you lose the championship game, good sportsmanship is trying to smile, . . .

congratulating the winning team, . . .

and making plans for next year!

When your friend gets the part you wanted in the school play, good sportsmanship is helping her learn her lines.

Congratulating the person who gets
the highest grade in the class is good
sportsmanship . . .

and so is not bragging if you come in first.

When you tell the truth about being tagged, that's good sportsmanship.

Good sportsmanship is not shouting, "Hurry up!" when waiting for your turn to roll the dice.

EXIT

STADIUM SEATS
A – D

And so is cheering for your friend if he
made the team and you didn't.

Good sportsmanship is not tearing up
your drawing if you don't win first
place.

If your guest wants to play Peter Pan, good sportsmanship is being Captain Hook—again.

And if your feet get tangled in the jump rope, good sportsmanship is being able to laugh with everyone else.

Good sportsmanship is finishing the race even if you know you're going to lose . . .

and it's being proud of a third place
ribbon.

When you think the umpire made a
bad call and you accept it without
starting a fight, that's good
sportsmanship.

And when your team loses because
the sun was in your eyes, you tripped
over a rock, and you weren't feeling
good anyway, good sportsmanship is
just saying, "I'll try harder next time."

A good sport is not only a good winner,
but also a good loser. A good sport is
always honest and fair.